BE KIND TO THE ENVIRONMENT

Coloring and Activity Book

Written by Barbara Feltquate
Illustrated by Lila Jones

To order additional copies of this book, contact:
Xlibris
844-714-8691
www.Xlibris.com
Orders@Xlibris.com
845964

5

6

Nature
Go outside and look around
All of nature can be found
Mountains and flowering trees
Wildlife, forests, and ocean breeze

Environment
The environment is everywhere
It is the land, oceans, and the air
Sunlight, streams, and skies of blue
Fishes, plants, and animals too

Ecosystem
An ecosystem is every living thing
People, plants, even birds that sing
Working together with all on the land
To keep the earth healthy and grand

Can you draw yourself on a branch?
Or something you feel or see
in the words of the poem?

Litter

Litter, litter is found...where?
In parks, on streets, even at the fair
Pick it up and toss it in a bin
Smiles and thanks you will win

Plastic Containers

Plastic containers are very unfriendly
A danger to animals on land and sea
Some think it is yummy food to eat
But soon discover it was not a treat

Can you draw litter to toss in the bin?
Or draw what you see in the words of the poem.

15

Plastic Straws
Plastic straws can end up in the sea
Tommy the Turtle found one accidently
While playing in water nobody knows
How a plastic straw got up his nose

Plastic Bags
Dolphins dive in oceans with joy and glee
Putting on shows for you and me
When one ate a plastic bag by mistake
He got a very bad tummy ache

Can you draw a dolphin and turtle with no litter
in the ocean and smiles on their faces?
Or draw what the words in the poem say to you.

19

Conservation

Take care of plants and trees
Animal friends, birds, and bees
Do not waste paper, water, or light
Try super hard with all your might

Electricity

Saving electricity can be a family game
Turning off unused lights is the aim
For every light switched off before bed
Place a yellow sticker on your head

Water

Kids can help save water too
Using ears and eyes to find a clue
Play detective to hear a drippity drop
Shut off the faucet to make it stop

Paper

Use less paper when you wipe
Try doing it with just one swipe
Start off with just a square
Saving paper shows you care

Draw something you see or feel
after reading the words in the poems.
Or you could draw something special
you wish to conserve.

Farming

Cows poop and give off gas
Hold your nose when you pass
They eat, burp, and pollute the air
Munching away without a care

Composting

A special bucket to throw garbage in
Becomes plant food when in the bin
Toss in a banana peel or an apple core
Even your broccoli that fell on the floor

Can you draw food to go in a composting bin?
Or anything you wish to create
after reading the poems.

Reduce
Reuse
Recycle

The 3 R's
While at school, at home, or play
What are the 3 R's kids learn today
REDUCE waste, REUSE stuff
RECYCLE when you've had enough

Recycle
Take something you would throw away
Change it into a new toy for fun and play
An egg carton can become a dragon fly
Can you think of another recycle to try?

Can you draw something kids can recycle?

Transportation
Do not use a car for a trip down the street
Put on your sneakers and use your feet
A bike or scooter will get you there too
Think about the environment in what you do

Pollution
Cars let out smoke from the rear
Slippery oil spills may appear
Chunks of plastic floating in the sea

Pollution makers...one, two, three!

Can you draw yourself on a bicycle?
Or something you wish to create
after reading the poems?

34

Plant a Tree

Plant a tree for play and show
Water it and watch it grow
Trees help clean the air
Helping pollutants disappear

Climate Change

Weather that shifts over time
Is the temperature starting to climb?
Sometimes these changes make us frown
Good news! We can turn it around!

Draw a forest of new planted trees
or draw what you see or feel
after reading the poems

Carbon Footprint

A tiny footprint shows doing good deeds
Thoughtfully balancing wants and needs
Using less energy is better for us all
A large footprint can be made small

Help the Earth in a great big way
By being kind to it every day
Remind grownups that they have a job too
To make smarter choices in what they do

If you wish, draw the outline of your foot
and then fill it with things
friendly to the environment.
Or draw whatever you see or feel
from the words of the poems.

The Begin

43

Printed in the United States
by Baker & Taylor Publisher Services